LOOSED

Stories in Rhyme

By Larry Davis

ISBN: 978-1545540442

Contents

Preface

LOOSED, *Stories in Rhyme*, has been a long time coming. The first story in rhyme was written in the late eighty's. When I wrote the first one I had no clue of the impact that they would have on people.

I'm eternally grateful for this God-given ability to express the thoughts and emotions of people from every walk of life, past, present, and future.

I believe that many of these poems are the untold stories of strangers, speaking and sharing their story. Some of the poems are biblically inspired, but give depth that could have only come from God.

A Special thanks to my wife Helen for all her support and love over the span of our 46-year marriage. To my children Angela, Mary, and Timothy. As well as my grandchildren Amia, Cienna, Malia, and Timothy Jr.

Additionally, special thanks to Caroline Meyers, my spiritual daughter and the inspiration for the first poem in this collection. Caroline, your sincere critics have been invaluable and are appreciated. You could not have been more passionate about them if you wrote them yourself. To Kelly Madison for listening with an open heart in all sincerity. The tears you shed in response to hearing each poem did not go unnoticed. To Mr. Alvin Davis, for inspiring me to take the next step and share these with the world. Your encouraging words were priceless. To Mara D. Johnson for her dedication to this project and tireless efforts to transition it from dream to reality. As well as a whole host of people over the years that encouraged me.

It is my sincere hope and desire that you enjoy taking a glimpse into people's greatest disappointments, their love, their hate, their moments of clarity.

Ca'line

A REQUIEM FOR A DEAD PROSTITUTE

Shuttled through foster care,
during my formative years.
Very little happiness
and a whole lot of tears

I arrived in Texas,
while still a pre-teen.
Already rough edged,
cynical and mean.

I dropped out of high school,
wanting a chance.
To make fast money
and decided to dance.

At club Savoy,
I danced on stage.
Losing my innocence,
at a very early age.

Yes before twenty,
I'd hit the fast track.
Flatbacking for money,
with tricks in the back.

Wanting to be loved,
I chased after men.
Trying to please pimps,
I plunged into sin.

I gave them my money
and got nothing back.
That pimps hate whores,
I know to be fact.

I was real dumb,
to say the least.
I gave more to pimps
and my quotas increased.

Then I met James,
an unschooled wimp.
But I turned him out
and made him a pimp.

For the very first time,
in my pain filled life.
I finally had a man,
who treated me nice.

I changed his attire,
down to his feet.
I'd never had a pimp,
to treat me so sweet.

But James had a woman
and a small kid.
But that square chick,
couldn't do what I did.

I made big money,
to put in his fist.
I wanted to show him,
she could never do this.

But he always went home,
to his square girlfriend.
The love I wanted,
I just couldn't win.

Things came to a head,
as I begin to make threats.
Of what was to happen,
if the two of us met.

James really feared me,
I see clearly now.
And plotted his escape,
the best he knew how.

James was no pimp,
beyond any doubt.
Just a square victim,
that I had turned out.

But I was determined,
to have this man stay.
No way no how,
he could just walk away.

But James was creative
and a cunning man.
And his fear gave birth,
to a master plan.

It's now so plain,
James never wanted me.
My life meant nothing,
if he could get free.

Oh my dear sisters,
don't be a fool.
Pimps don't love whores,
you're only a tool.

When you've finally tricked out,
to a broken-down hag.
He'll choose the square chick,
you'll be left holding the bag.

Hear this message,
I received from above.
You'll spend real money,
for counterfeit love.

A check cashing place,
James asked me to rob.
Without thinking twice,
I was down for the job.

This was my chance
and I wasn't going to blow it.
I loved this man
and now I would show it.

I'd get enough cash,
where we could retire.
To our own little cottage,
and warm by the fire.

This marshmallow dream,
the devil handed me.
Was only a plot,
for James to get free.

We arrived at the place,
on Galveston Isle.
Then parked in front
and sat for a while.

Our fellow passenger,
said from the back seat.
Don't send her alone James,
now getting cold feet.

James got angry,
I saw his mouth twitch.
Man stop worrying,
about this low life witch!

I wasn't offended,
not the smallest of shock.
Then James placed in my lap,
the nine millimeter glock.

I burst into the place
and shouted real loud.
Brandishing the glock,
at the terrorized crowd.

"Get down on the floor!
I'm not saying it twice!"
For anyone refusing,
it wouldn't be nice.

The cashier stood trembling,
her face flushed red.
Swinging the pistol,
I cracked open her head.

And I spied an old man,
from the corner of my eye.
Trying to crawl out,
of the door on the sly.

"You better stop Man!"
At him I yell.
I would have shot him
and sent him to hell.

I was already angry,
for blowing my case.
The broad I knocked out,
knew the key to the safe.

Left with chump change,
I raced out the door.
To find James had abandoned,
his unwanted whore.

Shocked and confused,
I fled on my feet.
This from my man,
I thought was so sweet.

Squad cars and uniforms,
I'm quickly apprehended.
And thrown into jail,
as James had intended.

I found out the place,
he took me to rob.
The owner killed others,
for trying the same job.

To add insult to injury,
the robbery location,
was only two streets,
from the police station.

Then from the court room,
seven years I faced.
I felt so humiliated,
ashamed and disgraced.

My grief was so heavy,
it could have been weighed.
Yes "Hollywood Meyers,"
had truly been played.

Looking for payback,
I paraded my anger.
A baggy pants butch
and baldfaded danger.

I became viler,
than the worst of my men.
And brutally forced women,
to join me in sin.

But women are twisted,
behind bars of steel.
The harsher I treated them,
the better they'd feel.

I finally realized,
I couldn't make them pay.
These sissified women,
loved it that way.

Rejected by my lover,
my life now a wreck.
I made a crude shank
and begin slicing my neck.

My wounds were so massive,
Blood from them pour.
And puddles around me,
as I lay on the floor.

My sin scarred life,
before my eyes flood.
As I lay there dying,
in my own life's blood.

But to my despair,
I fail the attempt.
God had his quota,
Like the rest of my pimps.

Let out of prison,
I'm back on the streets.
Not long after,
I'm walking my beat.

Parading my flesh,
down streets and lanes.
The devil then crushed me,
with powdered cocaine.

Where would it end,
I'd sunk even lower.
There's no place of refuge,
for a coked-out whore.

Big with a baby,
that I had nothing to give.
Eight months pregnant
and no reason to live.

But a man named Reggie,
began telling me.
Of a church on the corner,
where I could be free.

"The Lord's House Church,"
I passed one night.
And there out witnessing,
were the saints in light.

I went to join them,
out in the open air.
There on a back seat,
I sat in despair.

Their words had power,
as they testified.
How Jesus had saved them
and I openly cried.

I thought of my child,
I couldn't even feed.
Or even supply,
the basest of needs.

The preacher then told me,
his words were so nice.
I could be a saved mother
and give my child life.

The next Sunday morning,
at the alter I cried.
Where Jesus was born
and the prostitute died.

Just a month later,
God doubled my joy.
And I gave birth to Michael,
my fat baby boy.

Because for Christ Jesus,
I'd chosen to live.
A sanctified Mother,
to Michael I give.

I'm still at The Lord's House
and doing just fine.
Cause Jesus made a Lady,
out of Sister Ca'line.

A Heavy Heart

My heart was heavy
and grieved as could be.
I knew my wife,
was cheating on me.

We had been married,
for twenty-three years.
And now in this hour,
she brings me to tears.

I felt myself shaking
and raging inside.
The deeper I pondered
the harder I cried.

I found the evidence
while surfing the net,
the diary she'd kept
from the day they'd met.

The words of her diary,
penetrating like knives.
Words that would alter,
the course of our lives.

How she met him,
at a mall one day.
His charm and good looks,
had blown her away.

By now I was graying,
had gained a few pounds.
After eight hours working,
I came home and sat down.

I had worked hard,
to provide for my wife.
I thought she was happy
we had a good life.

A big fine home,
nice fancy cars.
I would even have bought her,
a trip to mars.

And now this pain,
deep in my gut.
All of my sacrifice
had been for what?

I read how she met him,
at Teasdale mall.
A muscular fellow,
handsome and tall.

The moment she saw him
she maneuvered her way,
determined to make contact
with him that day.

With arms full of packages,
she bumps into him.
At the touch of his body,
her head starts to swim.

He walks to her car,
they place packages inside.
"You can't let go of him,"
her insides cried.

She gave him her number,
he promised he'd call.
As all of her emotions,
were climbing the wall.

For twenty-three years,
I'd given everything.
Worked hard to provide,
to become her King.

But it all meant nothing,
from that very first day.
In her lust to have him,
she was throwing it away.

That call finally came,
to her delight.
They agreed to meet,
at a place that night.

They continued to meet,
he wined and dined.
That she was unfaithful,
never entered my mind.

It was not unusual,
for her to go missing.
Just more of her projects,
but not hugging and kissing.

But there it was,
neatly typed to read,
her inner most thoughts,
her deceitful deeds.

One of the things,
most painful to see,
her constant comparison,
of him to me.

I came in second,
in everything.
He'd stolen her heart
and now was her King.

I thought of those times,
she betrayed me with a kiss,
as she rushed out the door,
to their lustful bliss.

All the time styling
her big wedding ring.
As she flies across town
to the arms of her king.

My rage explodes
as I grab my gun!
I'll get me some justice
and to my car run

I back out the driveway,
a bad taste in my mouth.
Jump on the freeway
and gun my car south.

No way to stop me,
they both will pay!
I had decided to terminate,
their lives that day.

Hoping to find her,
in the arms of her king.
I'd shot them both dead
and take back my rings.

I fly down the freeway,
mouth filled with bile.
My rage was escalating,
with each passing mile.

Fussing and cussing
and shaking my fist.
Never once dreaming,
I could hate like this.

Rolling to their hideout,
I pass a police station.
But I drive right past it,
to my destination.

I found her car parked,
at the curb outside.
And wait til she comes out,
to get in the ride.

He walks out with her,
holding her hand.
I snapped in an instant
and moved for her man.

Finally she sees me
and they both run west.
As I'm pulling the gun,
hid in my vest.

I screamed at her,
"You cold blooded witch!
You've bought yourself
a six-foot ditch!"

They make their way,
to the police station.
Running full speed,
in their desperation.

They screamed their way,
through the station door,
and behind a counter,
crouched on the floor.

Into the station,
I too exploded.
My gun in hand
and fully loaded.

I see them there,
as they try to retreat,
and shot them both,
at an officer's feet.

As if in a trance,
he's sitting there.
As they both lay dead,
in front of his chair.

He springs into action
but slips in blood
and slides a short distance
and hits a wall with a thud.

Suddenly surrounded,
by screaming cops,
I raise my hands
and weapon drop.

At their command,
I fall to my knees.
They grab my arms
and handcuff me.

It seems I'm part,
of a docu film.
As I turn my head
and look at them.

All life now gone,
from her pasty face.
Her blank eyes staring,
off into space.

I wanted so bad,
to take my rings.
Her lifeless hand,
rests on her King's.

I want to feel sorry,
somewhere within.
But can't suppress,
a twisted grin.

They picked me up
and took me away.
As there in a cell,
in shock I lay.

I avoided trial
and copped a plea.
Twenty-five years,
they sentenced me.

For fourteen years,
I wore prison white.
While reliving the events,
of that dreadful night.

I can't let go,
the pain's still there.
Remembering her eyes
and their cold blank stare.

I feel no remorse,
I don't know why.
As fourteen years,
drag slowly by.

But one Saturday night,
as I sat in my cell.
A light came on
and I saw so well.

A veil was lifted,
and I knew that night.
To take their lives,
I had no right.

I remembered her pleading,
"Baby please!"
But shot her down,
upon her knees.

Her lifeless face,
I clearly see.
Her cold dead eyes,
now haunting me.

There on the cell floor,
I fell to my knees.
And ask God to help me,
to do something please!

I was filled with agony,
pain and sorrow.
But knowing I'd be going,
to church tomorrow.

I went to the altar,
when the preacher was done.
And God forgave me,
in the name of his Son.

I received Jesus Christ,
at the altar that day.
My pain and sorrow.
he wiped away.

Jesus has given,
to me new life.
And I've fully forgiven,
that man and my wife.

.

I made parole,
after one more year.
I have a new wife
and my own career.

I'm able to start over,
after all I've done.
Through God's amazing grace
and Jesus his Son.

Gold City

I came to Gold City
and settled down there,
with one dozen chickens
and a broken-down mare.

In rigged gambling halls
the streets were alive,
With pimps and prostitutes
In eighteen forty-five

I lived on the outskirts
in a broken-down shack,
kept my few chickens
and "old nelly" out back.

My father a trapper,
seeking furs all his life.
After mother passed on
took a squaw to wife.

When father passed on
and his squaw went away,
I cashed in our furs
and moved here to stay.

Now in Gold City
in awe of the sights,
drinking in bars
and whoring all night.

It wasn't very long
my money was gone,
I'd have to find work
or be forced to move on.

I didn't want to trap
for furs anymore.
I wanted to settle down,
maybe shack with a whore.

I signed on with the sheriff,
with his arthritic hands.
Soon asked by the Mayor
to replace the man.

As Gold City's sheriff
I had gained prestige,
but skyrocketing crime
had the city under siege.

I took on the vices
and didn't back down.
Even forced whore houses,
to the back side of town.

I then forced the gamers
to fix their roulettes.
So a man had fair chance
when placing his bet.

Found some young men,
whom I deputized.
As we began to bring order
before the town's eyes.

But as we made inroads
into law and order,
our town was invaded
by Mr. Drew slaughter.

A man from the Badlands,
a real outlaw.
A well-known gunfighter,
lighting fast on the draw.

This man had killed many,
gun downed in the streets.
And a half dozen lawmen,
patrolling their beats.

All of my deputies
when news got around,
turned in their badges
and rode out of town.

I alone was left,
to deal with this man.
I developed a twitch
and trembling of hands

My father had taught me,
a man faced his fear.
I had to face slaughter,
if it ends my career.

I could not run
and remain a man.
Though my deputies fled,
I was constrained to stand.

I knew in a shootout,
I would not win.
This man had gun down,
twenty-two men.

The man put bullets,
between their eyes.
From fast deadly shooting,
his opponents all died.

Drew would challenge me
I knew beyond doubt
and I knew that no one
in town would help out.

Alone at night
as the time drew near,
I asked God to help me
to control my fears.

The years of my life
Now seemed so few
So young to be dying
At age thirty-two

There would be nothing
To mark my life
No one with my name
No children or wife

I had no real home
and no one to care.
Just my few chickens
and my broken-down mare.

And now they too,
would be taken from me.
I wondered when it ended,
whose they would be?

I had lost my appetite
and had no real drive.
If I rode out on Nelly,
at least I'd survive.

Why should I die,
for a town that won't fight?
These thoughts were alive,
in my head at night.

The pressure increased
till finally one night,
I went to the preacher
and got my heart right.

I confessed to God,
the wrongs I'd done.
And I was forgiven
in the name of his Son.

Jesus came in
and my fears were gone.
I no longer felt pressure,
to ride out and move on

I began to praise Jesus,
down on my knees.
God sent His Spirit
and baptized me.

The very next morning
As it dawned toward light
Drew sent me a challenge
To meet him and fight

The town had two bosses,
there could be only one.
Meet him at noon day
or tuck tail and run.

I was so shaken,
it was hard to breathe.
I cried out to God
and fell to my knees.

"Lord in a gunfight,
you know I won't win.
I ask you to fix this
and strengthen me again"

Again I felt peace.
It would be alright.
My soul would be well,
If I died in this fight.

I went out at noon,
to walk my beat.
Prepared to face death,
when the two of us meet.

My hands were still shaking,
but my heart was at rest.
As I felt God's love,
abide in my chest.

I saw Drew Slaughter,
take a stand in the street.
The man that I'd dreaded,
I now had to meet.

I walked out to meet him
and his stone-cold face.
As I thanked God again,
for tasting His grace.

"I go out to meet him,
Lord in your name!
You said that I do not
bear the sword in vain

I don't want to kill him
or have him kill me
But I know in your name
I have victory!"

A metallic like taste,
had now filled my mouth.
A part of me wanting,
to turn and run south.

But I took a stand,
Gold City was my beat.
And I wouldn't back down
one step to retreat.

The man pulled his pistol
and aimed at my head.
I knew the next instant
that I would be dead.

But an invisible hand,
I felt pushing me down.
As I fired off my shot
and then hit the ground.

Drew's shot had missed me
But I struck his arm,
Other than that
He suffered no harm.

When the dust had settled,
I was left alive.
Falling down on my knees,
thanking God I'd survived

I was Gold City's sheriff,
for the next twenty years.
By the love of Christ Jesus,
I conquered my fears.

In eighteen ninety-six,
I departed this life.
Leaving behind two children,
a home and a wife.

If you love Jesus
and your heart is true,
in that real "Gold City"
one day I'll meet you!

Tina Faye

There was no peace,
for me Tina Faye.
A burned-out crack addict
and teen run away.

Back at my home
not enough space,
my brothers and sisters
all over the place.

My mama diabetic
and daddy a bum.
Fussing and cussing
and drinking cheap rum.

I finally decided,
I had to get away.
Things were too bad,
I no longer could stay.

Then I met Jeffrey,
boy was he cute.
Big body Benz
and tailor made suits.

I left with him,
with the clothes on my back.
A short time later,
I first tried crack.

I took that first hit
and fell back on the bed.
That explosion of pleasure,
from my feet to my head.

Like nothing I'd known
in my wildest dreams,
that liquid rush
and pleasure supreme.

From that point on
I was hooked to the core,
like ecstasy poured out
and I had to have more.

He always had rocks
and I smoked them free.
"The Candy Man baby,"
he'd say to me.

Then it happened
Jeffrey told me one day,
"I can't keep giving
these rocks away.

It costs me money
each time you smoke."
He knows I'm hooked
and stone cold broke.

I was truly addicted
and had to get high.
Realizing "my Candy Man"
had sold me a lie.

Asking of Jeffrey
"What can I do?"
"No problem baby,
for a looker like you."

"Plenty of money
out on the block,
tricks coming by
around the clock."

"Me be a prostitute
baby no way!"
But my old friend crack,
would have final say.

My very first customer
was a dirty old man,
touching my body
with cold wrinkled hands.

I felt so unclean
as I lay there in shame,
a big-time loser
in the "Candy Man's" game.

My soul enslaved
for hours on end,
Jeffrey would sell me
to streams of men.

Debasing myself
for pieces of crack,
the "Candy Mans" reward
for working flat back.

When I would get angry
and threaten to leave,
he knew I was strung out
and didn't believe.

I was a slave
to the "Candy Man's" play.
My innocence lost
and hope stripped away.

But Jeffrey went to prison
for a long, long time,
I was now on my own
without one dime.

My craving for crack
had really now grew,
one sure way to get it
I already knew.

There in the crack houses
doing lewdest of acts,
I did the unmentionable
for pieces of crack.

By age twenty-five
I was totally debased.
My life was a disaster
and gone to waste.

I'd recall my childhood
and often think back,
to the days before Jeffrey
introduced me to crack.

And wished that young girl
had really understood,
the life she disdained
had really been good.

That girl had been loved
by her crowded household,
not like these streets
where everyone's cold.

Crack has destroyed
a once pretty girl,
my hair now thin
had been full of curls.

I look like a scarecrow
but I'm not what you see,
that "monster" called crack
has done this to me.

Ashamed to go home
and show them my state.
That crack is now master
my future, my fate.

No longer marketable
out on the blocks,
I visited the crack dens
and begged men for rocks.

They did things to me,
they wouldn't with spouses.
I was treated like trash,
in the devil's crack houses.

Deeper and deeper
and further I descend,
the Lord alone knew
where this would end.

Kicked out of a crack house
after having a fight.
I cried out to God
in an alley one night.

Depressed and broken
without one dime,
I felt all alone
and deserted by time.

My reason for living
I asked the Lord why,
I was nothing to no one
and wanted to die!

If God is love
I just couldn't see,
why he would let Jeffrey
do this to me.

Then words from the Lord
drying my tears,
I'll never forget them
the rest of my years.

"Tina I love you!
And I too was hated.
Rejected by the world,
that my hands created."

"I've come now to deliver
to make you my own,
I'm cleaning you up
and sending you home."

Noise of a church service
I heard so clear,
the message about Jesus
pulling me near.

Just around the corner
there under a light,
twenty beautiful people
were worshipping that night.

I felt such conviction
as the altar call was made,
I fell to my knees
and to the Lord prayed.

I asked God's forgiveness
for my life of sin,
and freedom from crack
to start life again.

That night Jesus saved me
and delivered me too.
Freed me from crack
and made me brand new.

Three years later
I met brother Ron,
a man of great faith
and in love with God's Son.

The dear brother gave
delight to my soul,
we decided to marry
and together grow old.

I knew we'd form
a threefold cord,
with Ron as my husband
and Jesus as Lord

We said our vows
under the same street light,
where I first met Jesus
that fateful night.

No happier couple
than Ron and me,
my true "Candy Man"
and sweet as can be.

My hatred of Jeffrey,
has come to an end.
And fellowship with family
is now mine again.

Yes the Lord Jesus
has given me back,
hope for the future
and freedom from crack.

The Row

I've spent many years
here on death row,
all appeals wasted
it's time that I go.

Lethal injection
I'm facing tonight,
as the hour approaches
I'm tasting real fright.

I thought to myself
it's all just as well,
I'm already dead
here locked in this cell.

Twenty-two hours
caged up each day,
an hour for hygiene
and an hour to play.

There's not much to do
inside our little cages,
pick up a magazine
and thumb through its pages.

Then after a while
turn on the TV,
or do correspondence
to earn a degree.

With years to bond
here on The Row,
details of each life
we've come to know.

We file appeals
build up false hopes,
then turn to each other
for ways to cope.

The worst time for us
we've come to learn,
they take one away
and he doesn't return.

Helplessly watching
on his final day,
our brother, our comrade
being led away.

What do you say
as a man walks the aisles,
most hold their peace
and offer fake smiles.

What life he has left
will come to an end,
we'll get the news
we've lost our friend.

The Row alone knows,
the pain of it all.
As some sit silent
and some of us bawl.

Sometimes I wonder
if it wouldn't be right,
they blow our brains out
in the quiet of night?

In some cruel way
you see death as a friend,
knowing you'll never
see sunshine again.

Three or four times
with a man they'll play,
strap him to the gurney
then grant him a stay.

Is this really life,
to exist in a cage?
At times overwhelmed,
with festering rage.

The court appeals system
grinding ever so slow,
as you rot away daily
as a guest on The Row.

We've committed our crimes
in swift violent acts,
with years of slow death
the state pays us back.

Extending false hope
we'll win an appeal,
when everyone knows
our fate is sealed.

You say stop appealing
and just let it go,
but we all have a fear
of what's waiting below.

One day the new Chaplain
came to my cell,
who spoke words of comfort
then bid farewell.

I felt such power
as he spoke of the Lord.
I truly felt different,
that night on the ward

I waited impatiently
to see him again,
after a few visits
he seems an old friend.

His smile and bright eyes
brought comfort to me,
as he said in Christ Jesus
I could be free.

I told him I was sorry
for the man I'd killed.
When I committed a robbery
while drunk and drug filled.

He left me some literature
to read about Christ
and what it would mean
if I gave him my life.

How that his blood
would cleanse me of sin,
as I entered eternity
He would welcome me in.

But I really had problems
with this God that knew all,
why had he not answered
those times that I called.

Cause he had to know
if what they say is real,
it was never my intent
that night to kill.

He had to be aware
when I shot that man,
things had gone crazy
and it wasn't my plan.

How could he let them?
Is what I don't see,
strap me to a gurney
and put poison in me.

Was that really justice
when he knew what I meant,
how things had exploded
into a giant accident.

Why couldn't this God
if he controls it all,
just commute me to life
behind prison walls.

But I picked up the Bible
and began to read,
how god gave instructions
to Noah and his seed.

In Genesis chapter nine,
I read where God said
if you shed man's blood
your own will be shed.

As I gave it thought
I began to understand,
it hadn't been God
who put the gun in my hand.

In a drug induced stupor,
I entered that place.
And after a brief struggle,
shot the clerk in the face.

It was me Charles Ray
who took that man's life.
Robbing his parents,
his children and wife.

I saw it was justice
for them if I paid
and fell to my knees
and to the Lord prayed.

I asked the Lord God,
to forgive what I'd done.
And sought him for mercy,
in the name of His Son.

At that very moment
Jesus gave me His peace.
He baptized my soul
and my guilt released.

I told all my comrades
what had just taken place,
they knew it was real
by the look on my face.

The next time the Chaplain
came to see me again,
I asked him to baptize me
for the remission of sins.

I have the Lord Jesus
alive in my heart
and know I'm prepared
this life to depart.

The day finally came,
when I took my last walk,
they gave their smiles
but few of them talk.

What they were feeling
I knew ever so well,
leaving my comrades
in their own private hells.

We arrived at the chamber
they escorted me in,
strapped to the gurney
the execution begins.

They open the curtains
and people are there.
They all look somber
as they silently stare.

Asked if I had a statement
I nodded my head
"I love you Lord Jesus!"
last words that I said.

They started the injections
now angels I see,
surrounding my table
and smiling at me.

Blinding white lights
explode inside my mind,
as I leave prison walls
and The Row behind.

That glorious city
for me now awaits,
as I catch a glimpse
of those pearly gates.

I enter into them
and there I see,
the face of my savior
whose arms welcome me.

Adam

At the dawn of creation
I was fashioned by God,
who created my body
from dust and sod.

The heaven and earth
was all brand new,
as the first living soul
I was part of it too.

I had no mother,
no children or wife.
When he breathed into me,
the breath of my life.

At instant of consciousness,
I looked around in awe.
I could never describe,
the beauty I saw.

Eastward in Eden
God gave me there,
an exotic garden
to dress and take care.

It was true paradise
and contained every tree,
that was good for food
and pleasant to see.

The tree of knowledge
and the tree of life too,
there in my paradise
the both of them grew.

I was free to eat
of all the trees,
but the tree of knowledge
God kept from me.

I was not to eat of it
He then told me why,
"For the day that you do,
you surely will die!"

Yes I was the son
of the Father of life.
Who poured out His Spirit
on my paradise.

Then God decided,
I should not be alone.
He'd make an help meet,
to share my new home.

I was then put to sleep,
by the God of all grace.
As the very first surgery,
was about to take place.

He caused me to slumber
took a rib from my side
and fashioned from it
my lovely new bride.

None so beautiful
as this woman my wife,
who remained at my side
the rest of my life.

no way to describe her
a sight beyond name
we both were naked
and had no shame

Eve is the name
I gave to my bride,
but also called woman
for she came from my side

our life in paradise
grew sweeter each day
while dressing the garden
we'd run and play.

But one more subtle
than any beast of the field,
deceived my wife
into doing his will.

When he lead her to eat
of the forbidden tree,
she took of its' fruit
and returned to me.

Walking right up
placing fruit in my hand,
"Eat of it Adam!"
She then demands.

"Adam you see
that I'm not dead,
my eyes came open
as the serpent said!"

I looked from her
to the fruit in my hand,
dazed and confused
by Eve's demands.

I was God's son
and knew what He said,
as a battle now rages
deep in my head.

This thing called death
it was plain to see,
had not changed Eve
who stood before me.

Every living creature
stood perplex and still.
Would I honor my God
or do Eve's will?

Yes every beast
and all the fowls too,
all of them watching
to see what I'd do.

I wanted to please both,
but didn't know how.
For the very first time,
sweat beaded my brow.

I'm sorry my children
I made the wrong choice,
siding with Eve
I obeyed her voice.

As I lifted the fruit
to finally bite down,
the serpent stood smiling
not making a sound.

I knew right away
I'd made a terrible mistake.
My bond with God,
I felt sever and break.

The fowls of heaven
beasts of the field too,
all backed away
and vanished from view.

I had brought death
to all that had life.
knowing we were naked
I stood shielding my wife.

Then quickly we ran,
into the trees.
And made ourselves aprons
by sewing fig leaves.

What would God say?
What would he do?
Saying to Eve,
"I blame this on you!"

But I had known better,
she was deceived.
And now there we were
hid among trees.

I'm sorry dear children
for making that choice,
as our knees turn to water
at the sound of God's voice.

The last thing I wanted
was to deal with Him,
stricken with terror
as we clutched at limbs.

"Where art thou Adam?"
We heard the Lord say
"Why aren't you showing
yourselves today?"

I called out to him
as we crouched in the trees,
"We knew we were naked
and covered with leaves!"

"Who told you that?"
He then said to me,
"Have the two of you eaten
of the forbidden tree?"

I should have confessed
our iniquity that day
and begged his forgiveness,
but instead I say:

"That woman you gave me
Lord before I knew it
had eaten of it first
and made me do it!"

"What have you done?"
The Lord said to Eve.
Who now was in shambles
and sorely grieved.

"The serpent deceived me!"
Eve replied,
"Said if I ate of it
I'd become wise!"

God said to the serpent
"You are cursed above all!
For this thing you've done
on your belly you'll crawl!

The Lord then turned
and said to Eve,
"I'll multiply sorrow
when you conceive!"

Then said that her seed,
would bruise Satan's head.
And that I with sorrow
would labor for bread.

The Lord continued
His voice more stern,
"From dust you were taken
and to dust you'll return!"

God took skins
to make for us coats,
the slaughter of lambs
and innocent goats.

I'm sorry my children
what more can I say,
as we both were driven
from the garden that day.

We watched sin abound
for hundreds of years,
when Cain slew Abel
it brought us to tears.

But in fullness of time
God sent a new Son,
who offered His life
to save everyone.

There on Calvary,
He bruised Satan's head.
And three days later
He arose from the dead.

Yes the Lord Jesus
gave up his life,
to restore to my children
my lost paradise.

Eve

In the beginning
God made heaven and earth.
The angels were awe struck
and shouted with mirth.

The earth was void
and lacked any form.
The deep being enveloped
with darkness and storm.

That was the evening
of the very first day.
As darkness saw light
and twisted away.

The Spirit of God moved
on the face of the deep,
it wasn't till then
that the Lord God speaks.

The angels were silent
awaiting the sight,
as God gave commandment
"Let there be light."

Then morning sprung forth
for the angels to see,
they burst into song
and shouted with glee!

It was amazing
and a wondrous sight.
As nothing existed,
in the heavens for light.

This was the beginning
of God's display,
the evening and the morning
of the earth's first day.

God made a firmament,
which we call the sky.
Waters above it
and some beneath lie.

Even until now
they remain that way,
the evening and the morning
of the earth's second day.

The waters beneath heaven
gathered into their places,
as the lands of the world
showed their dry faces.

He called the land earth
and the waters called seas.
Then brought forth grass,
flowers and trees.

I didn't see it,
but it happened that way.
The evening and the morning
of the earth's third day.

Though the heaven had light,
God wasn't through.
The sun, moon and stars,
He placed in it too.

The sun to rule the day
moon and stars the night,
still remain in their places
for our pleasure and sight.

Glorious celestial bodies
God made them that way,
the evening and the morning
of the earth's fourth day.

God made great whales
and fishes of the sea,
great fowls of the heaven
small birds and bees.

God gave them no roadmaps,
yet they all find their way.
The evening and the morning,
of the earth's fifth day.

God made living creatures
all after their kind,
the beasts and the cattle,
the deer and the hinds.

And every creeping thing
that dwells on the earth,
God gave commandment
to gender and birth.

God's crowning creature
the focus of His plan,
God gave the commandment,
"Let us make man!"

On the sixth day,
God made His man Adam.
Then took one of his ribs,
to make him a madam.

Yes my name is Eve,
your mother you see.
Adam lived alone,
till God blessed him with me.

Tall, strong and handsome,
the color of rust.
It was hard to believe,
God made him from dust.

The moment I awakened,
I saw Adam's smile.
Sat up and took notice
and stared for a while.

I truly loved Adam
right from the start,
the man had the keys
to the rooms of my heart.

Adam was tender
strong and kind
and I was so thankful
this man was mine.

This world God made
was ours to explore,
it's wonder and amazement
and excitement galore.

Hills and the mountains
great fountains and falls,
the valleys and rivers
God gave to us all.

Our Father loved us
and made paradise.
The Garden of Eden,
for the man and his wife.

It was so beautiful
and a river ran through,
trees for food
and the tree of life too.

The tree of the knowledge
of evil and good,
we were not to eat of it
we both understood.

Yes our Father made Eden
and gave it away,
it was ours to dress
to live in and play.

The two of us naked
but not really bare,
God's glory surrounded
and covered us there.

I was called Eve,
Adam gave me that name.
Also called woman,
because from man I came.

Each day we awaited
for God to appear,
as there in the garden
his voice we would hear.

The voice of our Father
sent down from above,
drawn by His Spirit
to be smothered in love.

We would come running
and skipping with glee,
Me loving Adam,
and him loving me.

Both of us breathless
we'd stand holding hands,
our Father from heaven
his woman and man.

It was true paradise
I so dearly miss,
the time spent there
was heavenly bliss.

But I noticed the serpent
was always nearby,
as the end of our paradise
was now drawing nigh.

The serpent approached me
in the garden one day,
"May you eat of every tree?"
He asks right away.

I said to the serpent,
"I may eat of every tree,
only good and evil
is forbidden to me.

We surely will die
God said that we would"
As I gazed upon it,
looking ever so good.

"You poor, poor child,"
I heard the serpent sigh.
"Don't you know
you won't surely die?

God forbids you to eat
because he knows if you do,
to know good and evil
will be given to you!"

He stood there silently
with a knowing grin,
picked fruit to give me
to lure me to sin.

I didn't want to take it
and inwardly fight,
but finally gave in
and took a huge bite.

It tasted delicious
as I started to chew,
then running to Adam
I gave to him too.

Adam stood silently
just staring at me,
I said "Nothing has happened
I know that you see!

Look at me Adam!
You see I'm not dead
my eyes are now open
like the serpent said."

Adam stares at the fruit
he's tempted I see,
then nods in agreement
as he takes it from me.

That was the moment
that introduced shame.
My man had now fallen
and I was to blame.

I then looked back,
the serpent still there.
He's bent over laughing
and dancing on air.

I realized by the serpent
I had been played.
As all of creation
we'd surely betrayed.

Left all alone
to face what we'd done,
as terror sets in
the both of us run.

But where would we run?
Where could we hide?
As I felt such sorrow
for the man at my side.

Knowing we were naked
we hid among trees.
Making us aprons
of large fig leaves.

Adam blamed me
and I did too.
Not knowing how to fix it
or just what to do.

Hiding in the denseness
the both of us cried,
knowing within us
that something had died.

My big strong man
would never be the same,
the bride that he loved
had brought him to shame.

Hid deep in the garden
we trembled with fear.
The voice that we dreaded,
we both now hear.

You've heard the story
I know that you know,
after hearing his judgments
from the garden we go.

I soon bore Cain,
and then came Able,
but the first sibling rivalry
made Cain unstable.

Because of his jealously
Abel was slain,
as the very first murder
was committed by Cain.

We were grief stricken
but God gave us Seth,
to replace our two sons
taken by death.

But God had promised
the seed of Eve,
would bring salvation
to all that believe.

My daughter Mary
that chosen one,
it was she and God
that produced a Son.

Who brought salvation
from the serpent's snare,
by going to Calvary
and defeating him there.

He redeemed us from
the serpent's hand
and gave me back
my big strong man.

I'm mother of all living
you know it's true
and that makes Jesus,
my Son too.

Yes I am your mother
my name is "Eve."
You'll find me behind,
the word "Believe."

Barbara Sandria

At Airline and Tidwell
I often would see,
a quiet young lady
and mother to be.

Early in the morning
just before dawn,
there in the shadows
with child to be born.

I came a few times
and wondered one day,
where did she go
when she went away.

How was she caring
for her baby inside?
Did she go hungry?
Was she still taking rides?

The more that I saw her
more bothered I became,
I wanted to meet her
to ask her name.

That she was sheep
was easy to see,
this quiet young lady
and mother to be.

Early one morning
as it dawned toward day,
"Lord let me help her!"
I silently pray.

She had never spoken
or given one smile,
yet I was touched
by her and her child.

There at the store lot
I was backing my car,
I saw her motioning
to me from afar.

"Someone's behind you!"
I heard her say,
and that's how we met
in the store lot that day.

"I really do thank you!"
To her I said.
I'd asked to help her
and she'd helped me instead!

That's when I saw it
for the very first time,
a smile so beautiful
it blew my mind.

We remained at the store
and talked for a while,
asking her questions
and enjoying her smile.

I asked if she'd eaten
"no", she then said,
I drove to McDonalds
and the little sheep fed.

Said she was Lillie,
from St. louis Mo.
We did some more talking
I then had to go.

She'd come to my car
to get off her feet
and I'd give her enough
to buy food to eat.

Each day she'd tell me
things no one else knew,
painting a picture
of how her life grew.

Her name is not Lillie
it was just for the game,
Barbara Sandria
is her God given name.

We'd talk of the Bible
shared things I knew,
she said, "One day
I'll go to church with you."

Each time I'd see her
she'd smile that big smile,
she'd come to my car
and we'd talk a while.

Then one day
she was not to be found,
the baby had come
and Lillie not around.

Then she surfaced
still smiling that smile,
came back to my car
and we'd talk a while.

"Larry" she'd say,
"How did you know?"
Her smile would turn on
and her face would glow.

Things I would tell her
from the gift He gave,
knowing she was sheep
and would soon be saved.

Then she told me
the state took her son,
little Jeremias
her blessed little one.

I knew she was hurting
and offered her hope,
quoting God's word
to help Lillie cope.

Then they came
and took her one day,
the police arrested her
and took her away.

I looked for her daily
nowhere to be found,
maybe she'd left Texas
gone back to her home town.

I kept getting calls
from Harris County Jail,
finally it hit me
she was locked in a cell.

She had been caught
in an undercover sting,
but said she was innocent
and hadn't done a thing.

She asked me to help her
to get out on bail,
I hated the thought
of her locked up in jail

Five hundred dollars
is what it would cost,
if she didn't get out
her son would be lost.

I called several bondsmen
the price wasn't true,
five thousand cash
is what I must do.

I didn't have the cash
or anything to sell
and poor Lillie remained
locked up in jail.

When I told her the news
she cried out with grief,
no words could comfort
or bring her relief.

"Larry please help me!
Larry can't you see?
My baby Jeremias
will be taken from me!"

I knew his will
was not to get her out,
he had his reasons
I had no doubt.

Our phone call ended
timed out for the day,
but the cries of poor Lillie
would not go away.

The next day came
and I dreaded to see,
that inmate number
on my Caller I.D.

But this wasn't Lillie
sweet voice of relief,
"I prayed to God
and He's given me peace!"

Seems all of her grief
had melted away,
this was not the same woman
I left yesterday

She began to seek God
and prayed day and night,
asking him to save her
and help her do right.

I began to get letters
sometimes twice a week,
and then on the phone
the two of us speak.

She also wrote poetry
about her changed life,
now wants to get married
and be a good wife.

She also thanked God
He made me her friend,
she now had light
where darkness had been.

That someone had come
when she didn't have a dime,
showing Christ's love
not asking to spend time.

Her court date was coming
she asked I be there,
there was no one else
who even would care.

The truth be told
I didn't want to see,
Lillie chained up
and marched before me.

The day finally came
and I did attend.
And after a few cases
county inmates marched in.

I expected to see her
with a bowed down head,
but her face was glowing
with a big grin instead.

Hands cuffed behind her
she couldn't even wave,
but one look at her face
and I knew she'd been saved.

She became a new creature
when Jesus came in
and there stood a lady
where a hooker had been.

She looked so beautiful
my heart swelled with pride,
because Barbara now lives
and Lillie has died.

Yes each time I think of her
I'm almost in tears,
because the prostitute died
and Barbara now lives.

Noah

From the fall of Adam
things had gotten worse.
The Earth and inhabitants
brought under the curse.

Violence and murder
and hatred increased.
Infecting all men,
from greatest to least.

For the God of creation,
men had lost fear.
And moved Him to judgement,
in my six hundredth year.

Because men refused,
to honor Him as King.
God would destroy,
every living thing.

I preached to them
and pleaded too.
Giving them warning,
of what God would do.

But none gave heed
and kept their own way.
As we swiftly approached,
that great and dark day.

To build a great ark,
was God's instruction.
Giving me the pattern,
for its mammoth construction.

Thirty cubits high
and fifty cubits wide.
Three hundred cubits long,
with a door in its side.

Make it three stories,
with a window on high.
Having rooms within
and a vast food supply.

The clean beast by sevens
the rest by twos bring,
to keep seed alive
of every living thing.

I was to enter,
my sons and our wives,
God showing me grace
by sparing their lives.

The end finally came,
God said it's enough.
"Noah stop preaching,
gather your family and stuff."

"I'm bringing an end
to both beast and man,
this constant violence
was never my plan."

"You have I seen righteous
no others are clean,
the rest are corrupt
all violent and mean."

God urged us to hurry
to all enter in,
by a rain of forty days
He would wash away sin.

We all made haste,
to enter the ark,
as storm clouds gathered
ominous and dark.

We'd never more see,
the world that we knew.
As God shut the door,
it vanished from view.

It was hard to imagine,
they'd all be gone.
Save for our animals,
we'd be left all alone.

Because of men's hatred
their violence and strife,
He'd take from all nostrils
the breath of their life.

After years of warning
that day came at last,
once inside the ark
things happened real fast.

The heavens were opened,
the winds began to blow.
Great fountains of the deep,
were broken up below.

The rains came down,
increasingly they poured.
The winds howling violently,
in the darkness they roared.

The earth as we knew it,
We'd never more see.
Wondering among ourselves,
How the next one would be

.

We heard them screaming,
as we passed them by.
"Please help us Noah,"
"Don't let us die!"

But what could I do,
I was only a man.
This was God's doing,
didn't they understand.

I had tried to warn them,
I preached and implored.
But none gave heed,
my warning ignored.

Now God was destroying them,
not leaving a one.
From the waters of judgment,
there was no place to run.

Babies abandoned,
no longer mothered.
As the waters kept rising,
till mountains were covered.

God finally appeased,
His wrath now spent.
The destruction of all,
who wouldn't repent.

The heavens were closed,
the rains finally ceased.
The winds stopped howling
and their violence decreased.

God remembered the remnant
of those He created,
after one hundred fifty days
The waters were abated.

The floods receded,
The ark finally sat.
Coming to rest,
in the Mountains of Ararat.

We removed the ark's cover
and saw the sky.
God said we should leave,
the earth was dry.

I guess I'd best stop
my whole story you'll find,
in the book of Genesis
Chapters 6 – 9.

God made a promise
to never again,
by the waters of a flood
destroy all men.

When you see the rainbow,
please remember this rhyme.
No He won't use water,
but fire the next time.

Yes a storm is coming
If you will save your life,
Run into the ark of safety
Bearing the name of Jesus Christ.

Trick Baby

I was a trick baby
a product of shame,
never knew daddy
not even his name.

All my young life
kids have made fun,
talked about Mama
and things she's done.

I learned to fight back
even though I knew,
my mama was a prostitute
and what they said was true.

I felt like nothing
worthless at best,
I did poorly in school
flunking most tests.

Seems I was set up
to fail from the start,
I had low self-esteem
and very little smarts.

But I was a scrapper
and took nobody's stuff,
by the time I was sixteen
I was fed up enough.

I dropped out of school
to make my own way,
got me a trumpet
and taught myself to play.

Learned how to channel
my feelings through it,
as out on the sidewalk
for hours I'd sit.

made some sweet sound
real mellow and slow,
found I had rhythm
and was born to blow.

People would stop
to hear "Trick Baby" play,
blowing my horn
in my own stylish way.

The horn was my portal
to reach for the sky,
transferring my feelings
to those who passed by.

We two became one
the horn was my wife,
caressing her keys
and sound came to life.

Sometimes the two of us
will have small fights,
I'll stroke her keys
but she won't sound right.

We'll kiss and make up
she'll yield me her best,
the wind and the rhythm
explode from my chest.

The years of frustration
and rage she's tamed,
my mama forgiven
and no longer blamed.

Yes her "Trick Baby"
played trumpet so well,
at last I break the airwaves
and fan members swell.

I really gave thanks
to God all the time,
for bestowing on me
this talent of mine.

Born a "Trick Baby"
who seemed never to win,
but now I take comfort
in my musical friend.

I was now being paid
for what I loved most,
I didn't care about fame
or reasons to boast.

I just wanted to play
the thing I held dear,
to open my heart
and let people hear.

Then it happened
one rainy night,
as I stabbed my brakes
my car swerved right.

Losing control
as I made a curve,
my car spun out
and continued to swerve.

When I awakened
I couldn't even chew,
my mouth was torn up
and my teeth were few.

How could this happen
it just couldn't be,
why would my God
let this happen to me.

I scribbled my doctor
I just had to know,
would I ever again play
or be able to blow?

The doctor told me
it didn't look well,
my mouth was infected
and continuing to swell.

After months of waiting
several surgeries now past,
the day to unwrap me
was approaching real fast.

That day finally came
as I lay on my bed
and the doctor arrived
to unwrap my head.

He tried to prepare me
the best that he could,
but I wasn't worried
God was too good.

It was the Lord God
who gave me the horn,
I was destined to play it
from the day I was born.

His face saying nothing
as he gazes at me,
then hands me a mirror
and my reflection I see.

As I take a long look
my heart melts with grief
my mouth was disfigured
beyond all belief.

I'm just a "Trick Baby"
in this cold world again,
my mouth now wearing
a one-sided grin.

Like my whore mother,
God was just game.
I'm made once again
to feel so much shame.

How could he do this
He knows she's my life.
Snatching my horn,
my woman, my wife.

From that day forward
it was all downhill,
my thirst for hard liquor
became impossible to fill.

An emotional cripple
my mother now sick,
I cared nothing for her
and hoped she died quick.

It's all her fault
my "Trick Baby" birth,
conceived by a prostitute
and now of no worth.

Where are you daddy?
You fathered me man!!!
I'm the living proof,
of your one night stand.

Over and over
I asked the Lord why,
I was drowning in sorrow
and wanted to die.

Still carrying my case
and trumpet with me.
I tried with my sweetheart
but it wasn't to be.

I went to a pawn shop
and sold her away,
just like my trick mother
for money one day.

At the end of my rope
I fell to my knees
and asked God to help me
to do something please!

I felt someone touch me
and looked up to see.
A man with a Bible
and smiling at me.

Said that Christ Jesus
did really understand,
his face to was marred
more than any other man.

There in that alley
I fell on my face,
I cried out to Jesus
and tasted his grace.

I'm now a new creature
I've been reborn,
my soul touches heaven
and I don't need a horn.

God worked a miracle
given another chance,
I made peace with my mama
and headed to France.

There I had surgery
and in the mirror I see,
a perfectly formed mouth
there smiling at me.

Flying back to America
to where I was born,
there in the shop window
was "Trick Baby's" horn.

but I'm no "Trick Baby"
my Father I know well,
He loves me completely
and saved me from hell.

I'm in the church band
I have a real wife,
and making sweet music
for my Lord Jesus Christ.

I lift up my trumpet
and play Him my best,
as praises and glory
explode from my chest.

Sometimes for hours
on the corner I play,
to tell the whole world
that Christ is the way.

Gloriously Free

My head hasn't always
been messed up this way,
I'd been a professor
way back in the day.

I taught several subjects
small school in the south,
students were enlightened
by words of my mouth.

I enjoyed the night life
and loved to have fun,
I was single and educated
and lived on the run.

I liked fast women
but didn't want ties,
to get what I wanted
I'd tell them all lies.

A very nice dresser
and not into fads,
I paid good money
for everything I had.

I had the look,
of a man on the rise.
And saw admiration
in most women's eyes.

Young girls on campus
had me in sight,
asking for tutoring
at my home at night.

But I was no fool
and kept them at bay,
my record was clean
I'd keep it that way.

Then one summer
everything changed,
I hit on a student
and now I'm deranged.

Went out with Rhonda
who introduced me to "fry,"
got down with my student
and my sanity went fly.

She passed me the blunt
which was laced with wet,
my mind went tripping
and hasn't come back yet.

The devil used wet
that awful dark night,
replacing my sanity
with demons of fright.

That's why I'm always
moving around,
I know my mind's out there
somewhere to be found.

Behind voices that scream
real loud all night,
or in visions of terror
and unimaginable sights.

I spend my days
isolated, alone.
Still chasing my sanity
I constantly roam.

I know quite well
that I'm acting insane,
jabbering and chattering
things inane.

People are afraid
and stare in alarm,
they're all concerned
I'll do them harm.

But creatures of terror
are tormenting me,
my relentless enemies
that none of them see.

I know very well
I've become problematic
I tell myself, "Fool,
you're acting erratic."

"They surely will come
and get you one day,
put you in psych ward
and lock you away."

"You can't stand lock up
or being caged in,
their drugs and therapy
will start again"

Paranoid schizophrenic
the doctors have said,
cause I chase my sanity
to put back in my head.

Their therapy is wasted
because none of them see,
its demons and devils
that are tormenting me.

They prescribe me drugs
that make me feel dead,
weighed down so heavy
it's hard lifting my head.

I'm trapped in a world
that's beyond their scope,
I know the Lord God
is my only real hope.

And thank God one night
at a distance I see,
a man dressed in white
and gloriously free.

A Holy Ghost preacher
with his Bible in hand,
I knew right away
God sent this man.

The devils knew too
and trembling with fright,
they tried to force me
to runaway that night.

The preacher walked up
and gave a command,
"I charge you Satan
to loose this man!"

"In the name of Jesus
you demons be gone,"
as the devils were pleading
he leave them alone.

I felt the man's power
as a war raged inside,
the devils were fighting,
but he would not be denied.

The man kept praying
as I dropped to one knee,
the devils screamed out
and the last of them flee.

The mighty name of Jesus
had driven them out,
I've got my right mind!"
I arise and shout.

I felt so ecstatic
my mind was so clear,
I thanked god for the man
and hugged him with tears.

It's six years later
and I'm at home and wed
and no more devils
are in my head.

The Lord Jesus Christ
has put His Spirit in me,
I'm back in the classroom
and gloriously free!

Sinai

My name is Moses
a prophet of God.
To deliver His people
I was given a rod.

God sent me to Egypt,
with His rod in my hand.
To lead them from bondage,
to the promise land.

"I've seen the affliction
my people are under
and I'll bring them all out
by judgments and wonders."

"Going back to that land
you'll tell Pharaoh,
the God of the Hebrews
said let Israel go."

"That Pharaoh won't listen
I have no doubt,
but behind my judgments
he'll drive them all out."

The time finally came
that Pharaoh did cry,
"See my face no more Moses
or you surely will die."

I said to Pharaoh
"I'll see you no more."
Then instructed all Israel
to apply blood to their door.

for God had commanded
the lamb for the Jew
"When I see the blood
I will pass over you."

The night of the Passover
all through the land
the firstborn were smitten
by death angel's hand.

In every Egyptian household
a loud and bitter cry,
as all of their firstborn
drop dead and die.

Pharaoh and his people
demand Israel leave.
As he and all Egypt
are left there to grieve.

A night to be remembered
six hundred thousand men,
with wives and children
as our exodus begins.

Four hundred thirty years
at last we were free,
we came out shouting
and skipping with glee.

We worshipped our God
as our journey now starts,
He'd lead us to Canaan
and the land to us part.

God's presence among us
an awesome sight,
a pillar of cloud by day
and flaming fire by night.

Manna from heaven
God rained angel's food,
enough for His people
and the mixed multitude.

When God's people thirsted
He gave us a rock,
that gave forth waters
for the people and flocks.

But Pharaoh recovered
and came chasing us down.
All Israel was frightened
and running around.

We seemed to be trapped
walled in at the sea,
the people were angry
and screaming at me.

"Were there no graves
in Pharaoh's land,
that you've brought us here
to die by his hand?"

Pharaoh overtook us
by the sea that night.
The cloud to them darkness,
but God's fire to us light.

I spoke to the people
as I lifted my rod,
"Stand still and see
the Salvation of God!"

The Lord said "Moses
why stand crying to me?
stretch out your rod
and part the Red Sea!"

God demonstrated
His power and might,
as the waters erupted
and rolled back all night.

The Israelites shouted
and danced with glee,
as the waters stood up
and congealed in the sea.

Israel passed over
as if by dry land,
when last of them passes
the waters still stand.

Israel passed over
and turned to view,
Pharaoh and his army
come charging in too.

God peers from the cloud
the waters then fall.
collapsing upon on them
and drowning them all.

As promised to Pharaoh
I saw him no more,
his body now dead
on the red sea shore

Israel now knew
that God had all powers,
and the land of Canaan
would surely be ours.

Three months to the day
since we left Egypt land,
we came to Mount Sinai
and it's desert and sand.

Sinai's wilderness
was barren and dry,
we camp near the mountain
and God calls me on high.

He gave me words
for his tribes below,
that they were his chosen
they now should know.

I returned to the elders
to report what God said,
the people all trembled
and were greatly afraid.

"God will come down
to meet with you
and deliver his judgments
to his people the Jews"

"Sanctify yourselves
against the third day,
for God will visit you
in an awesome display."

"His words will govern
and sanctify our lives.
Wash ye your garments
and touch not your wives."

I gave commandment
from the God of the Jews,
any man touch Sinai
be stoned or shot through.

All Israel should come up
at the trumpet's sound
and to keep them at distance,
He made us set bounds.

Third day at morning
there descends a dark cloud,
the trumpet begins blaring
exceedingly loud.

As the trumpet grew louder
the whole mountain shakes,
our fear was so great
that we all fear and quake.

All of us awe struck
stand still and stare,
as Sinai belches
fire and smoke in the air.

Because of the burning
all of us choke,
Mount Sinai on fire
and bellowing out smoke.

When we saw the lighting
and thunder that day,
all of us fainted
and moved far away.

We then heard a voice
that buckled our knees,
the voice of Jehovah
now speaking to me.

"Come up Moses
I've called you alone,
to receive commandments
engraved in stone!"

Upon a stone tablet
hewn out by His hand,
God wrote with His finger
His ten commands.

I gave His commandments
to his people the Jews,
and all that He said
they agreed to do.

"The voice we've heard
has filled us with fear,
and never again
do we want to hear."

"Let his words be given
directly to you,
and whatever you say
that we will do!"

When they saw lightening
and heard thunder crack.
All Israel at Sinai
in terror drew back.

But Jesus has come
to give you Mount Zion
and invites you forever
to reign with the Lion.

In that city of angels
and justified men,
with Him that has washed us
and cleansed us from sins.

My name is Moses
the Shepherd of God,
and I'll see you in Zion
and show you that rod.

Glory

They called me big time
running back supreme,
no one my equal
the best ever seen.

This was my element
crowds screaming for me,
a primetime gladiator
on national TV.

The sound was deafening
as men would roar
and a house full of women
made noise when I'd score.

I'd take the ball
explode from the line,
before defenders reacted
the end zone was mine.

Down in the pit
the blood and the sweat,
defensive linesmen
I ran past like a jet.

Two hundred yard games
were normal for me,
on one of my good days
I was known to make three.

Faking and shaking
just like O.J.
I would give them a leg
then take it away.

Stronger than Campbell
and big Jim Brown,
dropped head on linebackers
and knocked them down.

Sweeter than Sweetness
and Emmett Smith too.
A real playmaker,
with monster reviews.

I remember what happened
in one crucial game,
defenders had vowed
I'd be coming up lame.

Determined to stop me
from scoring that day,
planning to gang tackle
on all of my plays.

Things didn't shake
till last play of the game,
defensemen celebrating
I had come up lame.

I then took the ball
on the very last play,
rounded the corner
and broke for day.

The arena was vibrating
with murderous shouts,
four men came charging
to put my lights out.

They all came at me
with murder in eye,
but my game kicked in
and I kissed them goodbye.

Running the ball
with grace and flair,
I left defenders grabbing
for nothing but air.

No one had touched me
when I crossed the line,
an eighty-yard game winner
the glory was mine.

The crowd was ecstatic
as they watched that play,
I had broken the record
for scoring that day.

Number one scorer
in all of the game,
had brought me glory
and worldwide fame.

I knew I would go out
with glory and cheer,
breaking all records
by end of career.

But things don't always
turn out as planned,
at the end of the day
I was not the same man.

There arose an opponent
I couldn't fake out,
he's called father time
and he packs real clout.

My legs weren't as swift
as they'd once been.
The blows I absorbed,
were doing me in.

My fakes too slow
oft stopped in my tracks.
When I took on linebackers
knocked flat on my back.

No heart for training
I was not what I'd been,
I knew in my heart
my career was at end.

But I couldn't let go
still longing to hear,
the roar of the crowd
the screaming and cheer.

Like Ali and Michael
giving one last try,
my dream was alive
and just wouldn't die.

But dreams and reality
told not the same story,
all left at the end
was a hunger for glory.

Demoted to backup
it became crystal clear,
my desire for glory
outlasts my career.

I'd wasted my money
all I knew was the game,
I was left with my pension
and a truck load of shame.

Starved for attention
but none to be found,
no one wants has-beens
hanging around.

Alcohol and drugs
were finishing me,
I was in a black hole
and no light I could see.

Then one night
at a seedy motel,
I cried out to Jesus
and to my knees fell.

That's when it happened
my shame was replaced,
by God's Holy Spirit
and His amazing grace.

The black hole is gone
new light I see,
giving glory to Jesus
who is cheering for me!

In the game of life
I once again run,
for the glory of God
and Jesus his Son.

A Soldiers View

I was despondent
and sore distressed.
The sights that I'd witnessed,
burned in my chest.

Jesus of Nazareth
a Prophet of power,
had died of crucifixion
within the last hour.

Trudging now wearily
back down the hill.
I was a washed-up soldier,
with a broken will.

A Roman Centurion
I had been so proud,
As early that morning
we'd held back the crowd.

It was the Passover
the Hebrews' feast
and the Jews were gathered
from greatest to least.

The priests and the elders
had delivered this man.
Raising accusations
and voicing demands.

A place called The Pavement
Pilate sat on his seat.
Intending with the priests
and elders to meet.

Who stood in the courtyard
and raised a great den,
sanctified for the Passover
they refused to go in.

Pilate being forced
to meet them outside,
they've brought to him Jesus
to be crucified.

They made accusations
of many a thing.
Shouting that Jesus
had declared himself King.

The leaders were envious
of which Pilate was aware,
"Take Him to the temple
and you judge Him there."

"This man is a malefactor
and we brought him to you,
to put Him to death
is not lawful for Jews."

"We would have stoned Him
this very same day,
But you Romans have taken
our powers away!"

Returning to his seat
Pilate sits looking grim,
But Jesus said nothing
when questioned by him.

"You give me no answer?
Don't you know I have power,
to have you crucified
this very same hour?"

Jesus then answered
As He stood in the hall,
"Without my Father,
You have no power at all."

Pilate cried out,
"Man don't you see,
It's your own people
that brought you to me!"

What have you done?
Are you a king?
Why are your people
doing this thing?"

My kingdom is not here
nor in this world found,
or my servants would fight
and I wouldn't be bound.

Pilate then left him,
and went back outside.
"I find this man faultless!"
To the mob he cried.

"But you have a custom
shall I release unto you,
in honor of the Passover
the King of the Jews?"

"Give us Barabbas!"
The chief priests scream.
"This man has a devil,
and He's nobodies king!"

Then Pilate beats Jesus
With a multi-lashed whip,
I was blinded with rage
and biting my lip.

A crown of thorns
pressed to His lobes,
as the soldiers arrayed Him
in a royal purple robe.

"Hail to the King!"
The soldiers then said,
Jesus now bleeding
from His back and head.

Jesus came forth,
bloody and worn.
Arrayed in the robe,
and wearing His thorns.

But the Jews are adamant
and want Him condemned.
Inflaming the crowd
to cry, "Crucify Him!"

"This Man claims
to be the Son of God,
you have the power
so do your Job!"

Hearing that Jesus
claimed to be Christ,
the Son of Jehovah
Pilate feared for his life.

"Who are you Jesus?"
Pilate demands.
"Give me some answers,
Speak to me man!"

When Jesus said nothing,
Pilate returned to the Jews
saying, "Jesus or Barabbas,
which will you choose?"

"Give us Barabbas!"
All of them scream.
"Then what shall I do
With Jesus your King?"

"Crucify Him!"
Of Pilate they demand
who delivered up Jesus
after washing his hands.

Had Pilate given orders
and authority to me,
I'd have scattered that mob
and set this Man free.

As I watched Jesus
my heart went out,
that this man was innocent
was clear beyond doubt.

He stumbled and fell,
from the weight of the cross.
His body being weakened
from the blood that He'd loss.

A large black man,
in the crowd I see.
The soldiers apprehend him,
and bring him to me.

We gave him His cross
to carry that day,
as Jesus arises
and staggers away.

Finally our parade
comes to a stop,
they laid the cross down
and placed Jesus on top.

The soldiers then nailed
His hands and feet.
The sound of the metal
as it pierced His meat.

The other two men
are writhing around.
But Jesus lay passively,
not making a sound.

I wanted to end it,
to somehow intervene.
Not wanting to witness,
any more of this scene.

When the crosses are lifted
and dropped with a thud,
their mouths scream agony
and wounds spew blood.

Their anguish is apparent,
in pain to even breathe.
No crueler execution,
was ever conceived.

The priests and the elders
strutted that day.
Feeling victorious
They'd gotten their way.

"He's saved many others,
but himself He can't save?
Didn't this fellow
Call men from the grave?"

They had a superscription,
hung over His head.
"The King of the Jews."
Is what the sign read.

"Father forgive them!"
He cries for the Jews.
They are blinded by Satan,
and know not what they do!"

One of the thieves
railed on Him too,
saying, "Save yourself
and take us with you!"

The other responded,
"Man don't you fear?
This Man is innocent
and shouldn't be here!"

Turning to Jesus,
saying "Lord I believe,
as you enter your kingdom,
let me follow you please!"

"Because you believe,
that I am the Christ.
this day you will join me
in my paradise."

As His agony increases,
we heard Jesus groan.
As if God turned His back
and refused to look on.

"Eloi, Eloi!"
We heard Him cry,
"Father you forsake me,
please tell me why?"

"I commend my Spirit!"
Jesus then cried.
After saying, "Its Finished,"
slumped His body and died.

The soldiers then seeing
that Jesus was dead,
as they pierced His side
He broke water and bled.

The stream of water
mixed with His blood,
ran down the cross
and mingled with mud.

At the sixth hour
as thick darkness sat in,
grown men began crying
and repenting of sin!

Large rocks were exploding,
all over the place!
As the earth then trembled
and shook on its base.

People were frightened
and running around.
I too was trembling
and fell to the ground.

Down on my knees
with my face in the sod
crying, "This man surely
was the Son of God!"

I left that hill
being wasted away,
knowing the Son of God
was murdered that day.

In Joseph's new tomb
they wrap Him with care,
intending after sabbath
to bury Him there.

The Jews sealed a stone
that none could get it,
that His disciples not say
that He rose again.

The women came running,
as it dawned toward day.
Astonished to find,
the stone rolled away.

Two angels in white
to the women they said,
"Why seek ye the living
among the dead?"

"He is not here,
but gone away!
Come see the place
where the Lord lay!"

"Tell His disciples
that He'll be there,
to meet them in Bethany,
they already know where."

The Jews started rumors
they knew wasn't right,
saying His disciples
had stole Him that night.

That Jesus is alive,
I know to be true.
As I received the Holy Ghost,
at Pentecost too.

I never went back
to the city of Rome,
I abide in the Holy Land,
till the Lord calls me home.

In Mark fifteen
Calvary made me alive,
in verses thirty-nine
thru forty-five.

Wade

Some people would think,
I had the good life.
A big new home
and a doctors' wife.

My husband worked hard,
at his nine to five.
And came home drained,
seeming barely alive.

I tried often to dress,
to ignite some flame.
But as the days rolled on,
it was all the same.

I wanted fast nights
and satin sheets.
A man who'd love me
and sweep me off my feet.

We would go dancing,
his arms would embrace.
While resting my head,
just under his face.

His breath would be soft,
on the back of my neck.
My head would be spinning,
I'd become a wreck.

But this doctors' wife,
is still trapped at home.
The truth be told,
I hated Jerome.

I often would ask,
but met his denial.
Jerome was opposed,
to us having a child.

Maybe if I'd had,
a daughter or son,
I might have resisted,
that low life con.

Wade was a knock out
with game supreme,
A fast talking hustler
stepped out of my dreams.

The moment I saw him,
I felt my heart race.
I got all prickly
and warm in the face.

My eyes locked his,
from across the room.
I felt the earth shake
and my pulse rate zoom.

He's headed my way,
I can't even think.
He negotiates the crowd
and hands me a drink.

I did need a drink,
my mouth had gone dry.
Wade was all that
and dressed so fly.

This man makes my blood,
run hotter than hot.
Wanting to fall,
into his arms on the spot.

I said "Girl it's not lawful,
to feel what you feel,
you do have a husband
and it's best you get real."

But there was no denying,
I wanted this man.
He asks me to dance
and I took his hand.

The music was slow,
I felt my heart throb.
My head on his chest,
as we danced in the mob.

His muscles like steel,
there under his coat.
I felt myself trembling
and a lump in my throat.

And like a rag doll,
I yield to his arms.
I'm totally wiped out
by his suave and charm.

I gave him my number,
to call the next day.
I had thoughts of Jerome
but pushed them away.

That night in my bed,
I tried counting sheep.
But my mind is on Wade
and I can't fall asleep.

His seductive cologne,
the feel of his arms.
That night I lay panting,
for his masculine charms.

Three whole days,
I wait for his call.
While Jerome talks drivel,
about a country club ball.

He was all hyped
and having a fit.
About me chairing the ball,
but I refused to commit.

I was most miserable,
both day and night.
I longed for his fragrance
and him holding me tight.

Wade's call finally came
and I wanted to shout.
All thoughts of committees,
was immediately tossed out.

Every chance I had,
was spent with him.
We'd go to the beach
and all day swim.

We'd sit by the ocean,
and take in the sounds.
The two of us watching,
the sun going down.

I spent all the money,
and wade spent none.
But I didn't care,
I was having real fun.

Wade began hinting,
if he had enough cash.
He'd blow this town,
and make a mad dash.

He'd move far away,
get a place of his own.
And he'd take me with him,
if I'd leave Jerome.

There wasn't much choice,
I'd never look back.
I'd be happy with Wade,
in a rundown shack.

This man was a tiger,
who met all my needs.
And I would do anything,
to help him succeed.

Wade constantly spoke,
of gaining a toehold.
And began asking questions
about Jerome's bankroll.

Jerome was a doctor
and had vast amounts.
And I had joint access,
to all his accounts.

We two got together
and cooked up a plan.
I'd steal Jerome's cash
and leave with my man

Not very long after,
we transferred his money,
to the offshore account,
of me and my honey.

No head for business,
Wade handled it all.
He handed me papers,
and my name I'd scrawl.

we packed up our things
and blew out of town
but found no real place
to at last settle down

It wasn't long after,
I bore Wade a son.
We called him Wade Junior,
after his father the con.

But Wade walked out
and left us one day.
Not even one word,
just vanished away.

I couldn't believe,
what Wade had now done.
How could he leave me
to fend for our son?

I had signed away all,
when the dust settled down.
Wade owned all the cash
and skipped out of town.

I entered a shelter,
a dank little place.
I avoided all mirrors
and the sight of my face.

I couldn't rebound
and stayed depressed.
Failing at jobs,
and neglecting my dress.

I loved little junior,
with all of my heart.
And wanted so desperately
to make a fresh start.

Its five years now
and I can't shake Wade.
This poor silly girl,
he really had played.

Jerome had remarried
and was doing just fine.
While I longed for Wade
and would just sit and pine.

But one night at a mission,
I sat still and cried.
A man preached about Jesus,
how he loved us and died.

When I saw the great love,
of the Lord Jesus Christ.
I knelt at the altar
and gave him my life.

Jesus made my old life
a new life again,
washing my heart
and cleansing my sins.

Unlike my experience,
with that con called Wade.
No chance in Jesus,
I'll ever be played.

Jesus made a new life,
for junior and me
and finally from Wade
this girl is set free.

Saucy

I still remember
that first sunny day,
as I sat there eating
at a sidewalk café.

I watched her pull up
in a cherry red vette,
remove her sunglasses
and then our eyes met.

My soul was electrified
by her stunning green eyes,
she was the big league
that blue ribbon prize.

Her smile like an angel's
but little did I guess,
it hid a high yellow serpent
in a skin tight dress.

She then takes a seat,
at a table nearby.
And a short time later
was joined by some guy.

I watched her in action
this guy was a toy,
she brought him to heel
like a young school boy.

She then turned her head
and nodded my way,
winked with a smile
and turned back to play.

I had known women
more than a few,
I took care of business
broke some hearts too.

I knew I had game
even built me a stash
and prided myself
on keeping my cash.

But Saucy was different
like none I had known,
I knew if I touched her
my game would be blown.

Like a wild predator
done stalking a meal,
she came out of hiding
and moved for the kill.

Walking right over
she pulled out a seat,
asked for my number
and if we could meet.

The fact that she did it
with the guy sitting there,
I knew she was heartless
and just didn't care.

Her eyes swept over me
in my expensive fly clothes,
gauging how swiftly
she'd put a hook in my nose.

She was so luscious
smelling ever so sweet,
my last ounce of game
dropped dead at her feet.

She said she was "Saucy"
her voice smooth as silk.
I melted like sugar
in a glass of warm milk.

I gave her my number
she said she would call,
I glanced at her fellow
no reaction at all.

That call finally came
I picked her up in my benz,
not long after
I let her move in.

From that day forward
my life rearranged,
the serpent invaded
and everything changed.

No game for Saucy
not even the least,
she led me around
like a four-legged beast.

Saucy threw tantrums
and foot stomping fits,
powerless to deny her
I was clay in her mitts.

She often degraded me
in front of her friends
and openly flirted
with nice looking men.

Went through my money
like a knife through bread,
I was grieving and hurting
but nothing was said.

In bondage to Saucy
my emotions flashed hot,
she had me all twisted
and tied up in knots.

She'd threaten to leave
and I'd beg her to stay,
but how much longer
could I live this way.

Then it happened
she came to our place,
pushing right past me
with a frown on her face.

Said she was leaving
with the man outside,
I fell to my knees
and with my heart cried.

"Saucy don't leave me!!
You know I can't live,
anything you want baby,
I'll work hard to give"

Knowing my bank account
was now all but drained,
she continued her packing
and ignoring my pain.

Watching her packing
I really got steamed,
my house had been paid off
but now had a lien.

Did she really think
she could just walk away?
That I'd let her leave me
in shambles that day?

She gave me a smile
and said I was nice,
but out of my league
and she had some advice.

"Please understand
you plain little men,
if you can't charm a snake
you don't take her in."

"I've found a new man
and that's how it is,
you don't have money
and I can't spend tears."

She then turned away
which made me see red,
I pointed my pistol
at the back of her head.

What did she think?
This high yellow witch,
my anger so hot
I felt my face twitch.

I said to her coldly
"Woman you'd best freeze
don't make me hurt you!"
But she still tried to leave.

I then pulled the trigger
and saw her brains splatter,
the door and the wall
now blasted with matter.

I thought of her flirting,
with all of those men.
And stepped over her body
and shot her again.

I turned my attention
to her man outside,
as I ran to the curb
he fled in his ride.

The police arrived
and took me to jail,
depressed over saucy
I cried in my cell.

I thought of her family
and hoped they would see,
I just couldn't handle
her desertion of me.

She ruins everything
and then wants to leave,
walk out with another
while I'm left to grieve.

That very thin line
between love and hate,
she had pushed me past it
that fateful date.

All I really wanted
was to make her my wife,
to show her devotion
the rest of my life.

she was the big league
that blue ribbon prize,
my yellow skinned darling
with stunning green eyes.

They sent me to prison
a hell hole of strife,
giving me a sentence
of twenty to life.

But I still love Saucy
she's alive in my head,
I spend my nights with her
on my prison bunk bed.

The years have gone by
her memory won't fade,
I'm finally released
my debt has been paid.

But twenty years later
it's still on my chest,
years couldn't pay
for my dear Saucy's death

I asked the Lord God
to save me one day,
the pain of my Saucy
to please take away.

Saying, "Lord I'm sorry
for what I have done
and I was forgiven
through Jesus his Son.

Time spent with Saucy
was one tragic mess,
but now in Christ Jesus
my soul has been blessed.

I know that I'll see him
one day in the skies
and lay hold on heaven
that only true prize.

Blinded To See

The nation of Israel,
God called to be His.
A nation of Prophets,
Priest and Seers.

Saul of Tarsus,
a Pharisee's son.
And my zeal for the law,
was second to none.

Taught by Gamaliel,
a Doctor of the Law.
His wisdom and teaching,
left me in awe.

I belonged to the Pharisees,
Israel's straightest sect.
Though still a young man,
I had earned respect.

There arose a Teacher
Jesus His name,
as Israel's Messiah
the Man had laid claim.

Masses followed Him,
wherever He went.
But the Man was unlearned
and didn't have a cent.

And the way of the Pharisees
He did not follow,
which proved His claims
were false and hollow.

Traditions of the Elders,
His disciples violated.
Which caused His sect,
to be reviled and hated.

He treated our customs,
as nothing to observe.
Till finally we're driven
to punishment deserved.

If we didn't stop
His theatrical sensations,
the Romans would come
and take away our nation.

We sought opportunity
to take Him by night,
away from the crowds
to avoid any fight.

Then came His disciple
and brought to us,
a way to take Jesus
without any fuss.

For thirty pieces of silver,
Judas betrayed His Lord.
And a short time later,
hung himself with a cord.

We then took Jesus
for Pilate to try
and loudly demanded
he condemn Him to die.

Hung between two thieves
at Calvary's Hill,
Pilate delivered up Jesus
to the Pharisees will.

He was not the Messiah,
it was plain to see.
The Law made Him cursed
when He hung on the tree.

After dying on the cross
and his body taken down,
All of His disciples,
then fled underground.

He was placed in a tomb
and a watch then set,
us Pharisees ecstatic
we'd stopped His threat.

It took three days
for a rumor to arise,
the man we'd crucified
had been seen alive.

The tomb had been opened
and no one was there
and word of this event
soon spreads everywhere.

Convinced His disciples
had taken Him by night,
we knew this rumor
could not be right.

The Man had been crucified,
we'd watched as He died.
Then Pentecost came
and they all multiplied.

The works that He did,
the Apostles did too.
Their leaders converting,
both Gentiles and Jews.

This had to be stopped,
we couldn't let it spread.
Some should be stoned,
the rest lose their heads.

The lives of these heretics,
meant nothing to me.
From this foul doctrine,
I would set Israel free.

There on my shoulder
the devil sat perched,
filling me with madness,
against the Lord's Church.

Both men and women,
I'd cast into pen,
and compelled they commit
the ultimate sin.

For worshipping Jesus,
they'd pay a great price.
Some with their limbs
and some with their life.

Breathing out slaughter
commanding they deny,
the name of this Jesus
or painfully die.

When Stephen their Deacon
was stoned in the street,
the witnesses all laid
their clothes at my feet.

My rage against Christians
was not satisfied,
with letters of authority
toward Damascus I ride.

Intending to bind all
I found in this way,
and bring them to Jerusalem
and there they'd all pay.

But there on the road
I saw a great light,
as we're all knocked down
by the glorious sight.

The men that I'd led
I trembled among,
as I heard His voice,
in the Hebrew tongue.

**"Saul! Saul!
Why persecute me?
To kick against the pricks,
is hard for thee!"**

Trembling and astonished
I covered my head,
"Who art thou Lord?"
To Him I said.

**"Jesus of Nazareth,
whom you persecute.
My chosen vessel
whom now I recruit."**

"What now Lord,
Would you have of me?
He said, **"Go to Damascus
and there you'll see."**

My eyesight was gone
to my surprise,
when I stood to my feet
and opened my eyes.

To a street called Straight
I was led that day,
and for three days there
I fast and pray.

Then this man
named Ananias came in.
I was baptized in water
and delivered from sin.

He restored my eyesight
but I'm thankful the most,
that Jesus had filled me
with the Holy Ghost.

I arose from the water
in Damascus that day,
that Jesus is Lord
I preached straightway.

I confounded the Jews
and taught from their law,
how Jesus fulfils prophecy
which many of them saw.

Saul of Tarsus,
I was no longer called.
But the Lord gave to me,
my new name Paul.

I carried the Lord's name,
among the Gentiles.
To Greeks and Barbarians
And the far-reaching isles.

Often thrown into prison
beatings above measure,
in reproaches and infirmities
I learned to take pleasure.

By day in the elements,
nights spent without sleep.
Thrice I was shipwrecked,
a night and day in the deep.

I fought beast at Ephesus,
and was imprisoned at Rome.
Assaulted in Macedonia,
and once I was stoned.

Five times I was lashed,
thrice beaten with rods.
To preach to the elect,
the mysteries of God.

I even wrote scripture,
to both Gentile and Jew.
And kept back nothing
that would profit you.

It cost me my life,
I have no remorse.
I fought a good fight,
I finished my course.

Yes thankful to God,
I shall forever be.
For blinding Saul's eyes,
to let Paul see.

God bless you children
Grace be with you all,
His mercy and peace
from your Apostle Paul.

Aroma

I was a victim
of raw circumstance,
born in the ghetto
with very little chance.

My mama a hooker,
and junkie for crack.
Who planned to kill daddy
if he ever came back.

Daddy left town
the day I was born,
with a high yellow stripper
on a cold winter's morn.

But mama took care of me
and did what she could
and made a safe haven
of our house in the hood

She really did love me,
I was the joy of her life.
I remember her kisses,
her smelling real nice.

But that pretty picture
would come to an end,
cause mama would fall
for a snake named Glenn.

Glenn moved in,
our lives turned around.
And the mom that I knew,
was nowhere to be found.

Introduced to crack life
she neglected her son,
hustling for Glenn
she lived on the run.

I learned how to fend,
Life no longer sweet.
Son of a crack fiend,
alone on the streets.

Life on the streets
was calloused and mean,
seemed no one had time
for sons of crack fiends.

Nickeling and diming
enough to buy bread,
while mama was chasing
more rocks for her head.

I was angry at Mama
and her parade of men,
tricks that she turned
for that low-life Glenn.

Why couldn't she see,
the man was no good.
Made me a laughing stock,
for the kids in the hood.

Glenn turned her out
my Mama was gone,
all but abandoned
I felt so alone.

I sometimes would hear her
sobbing to be free,
peering over her pipe
eyes yearning for me.

I would hear her sighing,
but no relief to be found.
The sounds of a crack addict,
chained and bound.

I wanted to kill Glenn
end his life for good,
but thousands more like him
reside in the hood.

We finally collided
at the age of sixteen,
I threw a left hook
and decked that fiend.

Glenn flew backward
from a blow to the head,
fell to the floor
lay there and bled.

Mama blamed me
for starting the fight,
and I had to move out
of her house that night.

I saw it coming.
I was so angry within
and had constant drama,
with Mama and Glenn.

Where was my Mama
who loved me so much,
her wonderful smells
her caring touch.

She'd now been replaced
by a junky dope fiend,
and I became hardened
brutal and mean.

I hated all women
and if I had my way,
I was going to get even
and make someone pay.

Now on my own
I get real on the streets,
getting down hard
with hustlers and cheats.

It didn't take long,
I had made me a name.
Soon rubbing shoulders,
with key players in the game.

I had big money
and drove a long ride,
nice looking features
and cocky with pride.

Pretty women everywhere
were giving me looks,
to be a true player
I had what it took.

I despised all women
and put trust in none,
remembering how Mama
had deserted her son.

Why they kept coming,
I never understood.
I showed no affection,
and meant them no good.

Just like my Mother
turned out for Glenn,
I played the same game
multiplied by ten.

I'd debase and degrade them,
but they showed no shame.
Professing they loved me,
as I called them vile names.

Some tried to tame me
and get me to wed,
I'd laugh in their face
and kick them from bed.

I was no trick
and couldn't be played,
Many passed through,
but none of them stayed.

I knew they would hurt you,
but getting there first,
I dished out a beating,
just shy of a hearse.

I still blamed Mama
where had she been,
kicking me out
for that low-life Glenn.

But it wasn't very long,
I was all burned out.
"Mama I hate you!"
I often would shout.

But for her sweet kisses
the smells that she had,
I still had a longing
and craved them real bad.

One night feeling lonely
I fell on my face,
and asked God to help me
my pain to erase.

That very next Sunday
I went to his house,
and sat in my seat
as quiet as a mouse.

Looking for help,
in the only place I knew.
My heart began breaking,
as I sat in the pew.

I heard how Jesus
betrayed by a friend,
said "Father forgive them,"
then died for our sins.

The preacher said, "Come,
if you want to be saved."
I went to the altar,
and there bowed and prayed.

Asking the Father
to cleanse me from sin.
Then opened my heart
and Jesus came in.

Oh sweet wonder
I saw the light,
my hatred of Mama
just hadn't been right.

From all of my anger
my heart was cleansed,
and God sent his Spirit
to abide within.

No longer a player
I'm now for real,
I preach for Jesus
and love how I feel.

I prayed for my Mama
often with tears,
and we finally made up
after many, many years.

And glory to God,
Mama too got saved.
Delivered from crack,
before seeing her grave.

Because of his mercy,
I'm treating her right.
We may have disagreements,
but we never have fights.

Jesus made Mama
my very best friend,
the mom that I lost
I've now found again.

Once again I find haven
in my Mama's little home,
I moved in with her
and she's not left alone.

She once again smothers me,
with kisses so sweet.
Smelling like Jesus,
as I sit at her feet.

Thanks to Christ Jesus,
and his Father above.
I'm now born again,
and the son of his love.

The Supreme Ruler

The masses were blinded
and didn't understand,
The true intentions
of this sinister man.

For this was the one
who had been foretold,
all through the Bible
by prophets of old.

A man of dark powers
his origins unknown,
soon conquered the earth
and made it his own.

The beast of perdition,
the devil's own son.
Unleashed nuclear horrors,
and left the world stunned.

World famous cities,
lying barren and waste.
Causes strongest of nations,
to surrender in haste.

Void of conscience,
A demon disguised.
He declares himself Lord,
of earth and skies.

He wrote his own laws,
and none gave flack.
His nuclear savagery,
laid the world on its back.

He now stood alone,
as Ruler Supreme.
And used his false prophet,
to run his regime.

All was now his,
to pillage and plunder.
He decimates the earth,
and plows the world under.

Placing in authority,
the vilest of men.
He raised stiff taxes
and gave license to sin.

Global Tracking systems,
hurling through space.
His eyes kept watch,
on the whole human race.

The masses adored him,
extolling his fame.
And worshipped the devil,
while showing no shame.

Men bowed to his image,
from greatest to least.
And all must receive,
the mark of the beast.

The world then watches,
on global TV.
As Christians are captured,
who defied his decree.

The beast was seething,
and shaking his fist.
Trembling with rage,
at those who resist.

His prophet sat scowling,
not the least bit amused.
This man breathed loathing,
for Christians and Jews.

For the Christian captives,
this was no game.
The beast was determined,
they'd worship his name.

But all of them knew,
ever so well,
to worship the beast,
would send them to hell.

Multitudes hated them
and screamed for their lives.
Betrayed by their children,
their husbands and wives.

Even their parents,
aligned with the beast.
Applaud their destruction,
from greatest to least.

The beast stood screaming,
"You all will die!"
As the false prophet arose
and called fire from the sky.

The beast was roaring,
his wrath engaged.
Fire falling around him,
accented his rage.

"I am the Lord,
you all will learn.
Those who defy me,
are destined to burn.

And now you'll bow,
here on the spot.
Or I'll have you slaughtered,
and left to rot."

Surrounded by fire,
his eyes sharp as knives.
The weaker saints withered
and begged for their lives.

"Fall down and worship,"
the beast then barked.
As they bowed in shame
and received his mark.

The beast in triumph,
curses the "**Lamb**."
And blasphemes the name,
Of mighty "**I am**."

But the strong refused,
to grovel and squirm.
Their love for Christ Jesus,
made them stand firm.

The beast now furious,
their tortured to death.
But still confessed Jesus,
with the last of their breath.

His wrath appeased,
The beast relents.
And once again smiles,
his rage now spent.

On Global TV,
he proclaims a feast.
They ate and made merry
and worshipped the beast.

"Who?" they chanted,
"Can war with him?"
But the **God of Heaven**,
soon answered them.

There at Armageddon,
the stage was set.
There the beast's challenge,
by **Jesus** was met.

With thunder and lightning,
the heavens rolled back.
As the Armies of Glory,
descended and attacked.

King Jesus himself,
was leading the fight.
The beast and his prophet,
He blinded with light.

His armies that followed,
made haste to retreat.
But destruction befell them,
as they stood on their feet.

Their flesh fell away,
as they turned to run south.
Eyes melt in their sockets,
their tongues in their mouth.

This was the **Lord's** sacrifice
and just as He said,
Ravenous beast and fowls,
did dine on the dead.

The beast and false prophet,
then faced the Lord's ire.
As He cast them alive,
into the Lake of Fire.

Forever and ever,
they both will burn.
That **Jesus Is Lord**,
they too have learned.

O'lord O'lord

This is murder,
in the first degree.
Heroin is slowly,
butchering me.

It's given me grief
down through the years,
now pus is running
from my ears.

For clinics and doctors
I have no time,
heroin forces me
to commit more crime.

I've got to cop
and cop real quick,
or it'll come down hard
and make me sick.

The air is hot,
it's late in June.
But I can't sit around
I must score soon.

A junkie fiend,
I do main line.
Death is surging,
in these veins of mine.

My arms are scarred
from years of smack
and all dried up
and covered with tracks.

I score the works
to ease the pain
and frantically search
to find a vein.

But they've all collapsed
from years of use,
nasty needles
and self-abuse.

I've had it man
I long to quit
and promise I will
after one last hit.

I tie my arm,
but no vein swells.
No place to inject
this load from hell.

No way to feed
this jones of mine,
this junk's no good
if I can't main line!

All I want
is to find a vein,
to drop this load
and avoid the pain.

"I promise Lord
it's my last hit,
I'll do this lick
and then I'll quit."

I said "You liar
you no good bum,
you know you'll slam
more death in your arm."

"You can't quit
you junkie fiend
you've been doing smack
since you turned sixteen."

"Junk's your boss
until you die,
he tells you leap
and you ask how high"

It's not right
to live like this,
I have no life
I just exist.

I need relief
and need it quick,
my melt down's starting
I now feel sick.

I regurgitate
against a wall,
a nasty bile
into which I fall.

I lay there crying
in this nasty mess,
in utter despair
I pray for death.

A terrible shroud
envelops me,
my life is death
and I can't break free.

But a man has come
and parked his car,
he doesn't belong
outside this bar.

He comes right over
and speaks with me,
said in Jesus
I'll be made free.

I receive his words
and feel so good.
They hear me bawling
throughout the hood.

I gave to Jesus,
my life that night.
And none that knew me
believed the sight.

I looked at my arms,
not even a track.
And no more monkey
is riding my back.

I am a new creature
I've been set free,
the power of Jesus
has rescued me.

O Lord! O Lord!
I see the light
and now I'm able
to do what's right.

O Lord! O Lord!
You saved my soul
and one day I'll walk
those streets of gold!

Dedication

This book is dedicated to the Glory of God
and our Lord and Savior Jesus Christ.

Connect With the Author

E-mail: LoosedbyJesus@gmail.com
Facebook: https://www.facebook.com/Loosed-326294607787305/
Church: https://www.facebook.com/TheLordsHouseHouston/
Outreach Ministry: www.thelordshouseoutreach.com

Join us in person:

The Lord's House
2501 McGowen St
Houston, Texas 77004

Tuesday: 7:00 pm – 10:00 pm Thursday: 7:00 pm – 10:00pm
Sunday School: 10:00am to 12:00 noon Worship: 12 noon -3:00pm